Samuel Rogers

An Epistle to a Friend

With other Poems

Samuel Rogers

An Epistle to a Friend
With other Poems

ISBN/EAN: 9783337006006

Printed in Europe, USA, Canada, Australia, Japan

Cover: Foto ©Thomas Meinert / pixelio.de

More available books at **www.hansebooks.com**

A N

EPISTLE

T O

A FRIEND,

WITH OTHER

P O E M S.

BY THE AUTHOR OF

"THE PLEASURES OF MEMORY."

LONDON:

PRINTED BY R. NOBLE,

FOR T. CADELL, JUNIOR, AND W. DAVIES,

STRAND.

1798.

PREFACE.

EVERY reader turns with pleafure to thofe paffages of Horace, and Pope, and Boileau, which defcribe how they lived and where they dwelt ; and which, being interfperfed among their fatirical writings, derive a fecret and irrefiftible grace from the contraft, and are admirable examples of what in Painting is termed repofe.

We have admittance to Horace at all hours. We enjoy the company and converfation at his table ; and his fuppers, like Plato's, ' non folum in præfentia, fed etiam poftero die jucundæ funt.' But, when we look round as we fit there, we find ourfelves in a Sabine farm, and not in a Roman villa. His windows have every charm of profpect ; but his furniture might have defcended from Cincinnatus ; and gems, and pictures, and old marbles are mentioned by him more than once with a feeming indifference.

His Englifh Imitator thought and felt, perhaps, more correctly on the fubject ; and embellifhed his garden and grotto with great

induftry

induſtry and ſuccefs. But to thefe alone he folicits our notice. On the ornaments of his houfe he is filent ; and appears to have referved all the minuter touches of his pencil for the library, the chapel, and the banquetting-room of Timon. Nor could the Diable boiteux have laid them open with more ability. Le favoir de notre fiècle, fays Roufſeau, tend beaucoup plus à détruire qu'à èdifier. On cenfure d'un ton de maitre ; pour propoſer, il en faut prendre un autre.

It is the defign of this Epiſtle to illuſtrate the virtue of True Taſte ; and to ſhew how little ſhe requires to fecure, not only the comforts, but even the elegancies of life. True Taſte is an excellent Economiſt. She confines her choice to few objeċts, and delights in producing great effeċts by fmall means : while Falfe Taſte is for ever fighing after the new and the rare; and reminds us, in her works, of the Scholar of Apelles, who, not being able to paint his Helen beautiful, determined to make her fine.

ARGUMENT.

AN

E P I S T L E

TO A

F R I E N D.

WHEN, with a REAUMUR's fkill, thy curious mind

Has clafs'd the infect-tribes of human-kind,

Each with its bufy hum, or gilded wing,

Its fubtle web-work, or its venom'd fting;

Let me, to claim a few unvalued hours,   5

Point the green lane that leads thro' fern and flowers:

The fhelter'd gate that opens to my field,

And the white front thro' mingling elms reveal'd.

In vain, alas, a village-friend invites

To fimple comforts, and domeſtic rites,   10

When the gay months of Carnival reſume

Their annual round of glitter and perfume ;

When Bond-ſtreet hails thee to its ſplendid mart,

Its hives of ſweets, and cabinets of art ;

And, lo, majeſtic as thy manly ſong,   15

Flows the full tide of human life along.

Still muſt my partial pencil love to dwell

On the home-proſpeĉts of my hermit cell ;

The moſſy pales that ſkirt the orchard-green,

Here hid by ſhrub-wood, there by glimpſes ſeen ;   20

                                              And

And the brown pathway, that, with carelefs flow,

Sinks, and is loft among the trees below.

Still muft it trace (the flattering tints forgive)

Each fleeting charm that bids the landfcape live.

Oft o'er the mead, at pleafing diftance, pafs '   25

Browfing the hedge by fits the pannier'd afs ;

The idling fhepherd-boy, with rude delight,

Whiftling his dog to mark the pebble's flight ;

And in her kerchief blue the cottage-maid,

With brimming pitcher from the fhadowy glade.   30

Far to the fouth a mountain-vale retires,

Rich in its groves, and glens, and village-fpires ;

Its upland lawns, and cliffs with foliage hung,

Its wizard-ftream, nor namelefs nor unfung:

B 2   And

And, thro' the various year, the various day ²,   35

What fcenes of glory burft, and melt away !

When April-verdure fprings in Grofvenor-fquare,

And the furr'd Beauty comes to winter there,

She bids old Nature marr the plan no more,

Yet ftill the feafons circle as before.   40

Ah, ftill as foon the young Aurora plays,

Tho' moons and flambeaux trail their broadeft blaze ;

As foon the fky-lark pours his matin fong,

Tho' Evening lingers at the mafk fo long.

There let her ftrike with momentary ray,   45

As tapers fhine their little lives away ;

There

There let her practife from herfelf to fteal,

And look the happinefs fhe does not feel;

The ready fmile and bidden blufh employ

At Faro-routs that dazzle to deftroy ;   50

Fan with affected eafe the effenc'd air,

And lifp of fafhions with unmeaning ftare.

Be thine to meditate an humbler flight,

When morning fills the fields with rofy light ;

Be thine to blend, nor thine a vulgar aim,   55

Repofe with dignity, with Quiet fame.

Here no ftate-chambers in long line unfold,

Bright with broad mirrors, rough with fretted gold ;

Yet modeft ornament, with ufe combin'd,

Attracts the eye to exercife the mind.   60

Small

Small change of fcene, fmall fpace his home requires ³,

Who leads a life of fatisfied defires.

What tho' no marble breathes, no canvas glows,

From every point a ray of genius flows ! ⁴

Be mine to blefs the more mechanic fkill,   65

That ftamps, renews, and multiplies at will ;

And cheaply circulates, thro' diftant climes,

The faireft relics of the pureft times.

Here from the mould to confcious being ftart

Thofe finer forms, the miracles of art;   70

Here chofen gems, impreft on fulphur, fhine,

That flept for ages in a fecond mine ;

And here the faithful graver dares to trace

A MICHAEL'S grandeur, and a RAPHAEL'S grace!

Thy

Thy gallery, Florence, gilds my humble walls,　　75

And my low roof the Vatican recalls!

Soon as the morning-dream my pillow flies,

To waking fenfe what brighter vifions rife!

O mark! again the courfers of the Sun, '

At GUIDO's call, their round of glory run!　　80

Again the rofy Hours refume their flight,

Obfcur'd and loft in floods of golden light!

But could thine erring friend fo long forget

(Sweet fource of penfive joy and fond regret)

That here its warmeft hues the pencil flings,　　85

Lo! here the loft reftores, the abfent brings;

And

And ſtill the Few beſt lov'd and moſt rever'd ⁶

Riſe round the board their ſocial ſmile endear'd ? ⁷

Nor boaſt, O Choiſy, ſeat of ſoft delight, ⁸

The ſecret charm of thy voluptuous night.   90

Vain is the blaze of wealth, the pomp of power!

Lo, here, attendant on the ſhadowy hour,

Thy cloſet-ſupper, ſerv'd by hands unſeen,

Sheds, like an evening-ſtar, its ray ſerene, ⁹

To hail our coming.   Not a ſtep prophane   95

Dares, with rude ſound, the cheerful rite reſtrain ;

And, while the frugal banquet glows reveal'd,

Pure and unbought*,— the natives of my field ;

* —dapes inemptas. HOR.

While

While blufhing fruits thro' fcatter'd leaves invite,

Still clad in bloom, and veil'd in azure light;—   100

With wine, as rich in years as HORACE fings,

With water, clear as his own fountain flings,

The fhifting fide-board plays its humbler part,

Beyond the triumphs of a Loriot's art.

Selected fhelves fhall claim thy ftudious hours ;   105

There fhall thy ranging mind be fed on flowers ! *

There, while the fhaded lamp's mild luftre ftreams,

Read ancient books, or woo infpiring dreams; **

> * —apis Matinæ
>   More modoque
>   Grata carpentis thyma—   HOR.

c   And

And, when a fage's buft arrefts thee there, ''

Paufe, and his features with his thoughts compare.   110

—Ah, moft that Art my grateful rapture calls,

Which breathes a foul into the filent walls ; *

Which gathers round the Wife of every Tongue, ''

All on whofe words departed nations hung;

Still prompt to charm with many a converfe fweet;   115

Guides in the world, companions in retreat!

Tho' my thatch'd bath no rich mofaic knows,

A limpid fpring with unfelt current flows.

Emblem of Life! which, ftill as we furvey,

Seems motionlefs, yet ever glides away!   120

* Poftea verò quàm Tyrannio mihi libros difpofuit, mens addita videtur
meis ædibus. Cic.

The

The fhadowy walls record, with Attic art,

The ftrength and beauty that its waves impart.

Here THETIS, bending, with a mother's fears

Dips her dear boy, whofe pride reftrains his tears.

There VENUS, rifing, fhrinks with fweet furprize,   125

As her fair felf reflected feems to rife!

But hence away! yon rocky cave beware!

A fullen captive broods in filence there. ' '

There, tho' the dog-ftar flame, condemn'd to dwell,

In the dark centre of its inmoft cell,   130

Wild Winter minifters his dread controul,

To cool, and cryftallize the nectar'd bowl!

His faded form an awful grace retains;

Stern tho' fubdued, majeftic tho' in chains!

Far

Far from the joylefs glare, the maddening ftrife,   135

And all 'the dull impertinence of life,'

Thefe eyelids open to the rifing ray, ''

And clofe, when Nature bids, at clofe of day.

Here, at the dawn, the kindling landfcape glows ;

There noon-day levees call from faint repofe.   140

Here the flufh'd wave flings back the parting light ;

There glimmering lamps anticipate the night.

When from his claffic dreams the ftudent fteals, *

Amid the buzz of crouds, the whirl of wheels,

---

* Ingenium, fibi quod vacuas defumpfit Athenas,
   Et ftudiis annos feptem dedit, infenuitque
   Libris et curis, ftatuâ taciturnius exit
   Plerumque—   HOR.

To

To mufe unnotic'd, while around him prefs   145

The meteor-forms of equipage and drefs ;

Alone, in wonder loft, he feems to ftand

A very ftranger in his native land!

Like thofe bleft Youths (forgive the fabling page) ''

Whofe blamelefs lives deceiv'd a twilight age, *   150

Spent in fweet flumbers; till the miner's fpade

Unclos'd the cavern, and the morning play'd.

Ah, what their ftrange furprize, their wild delight!

New arts of life, new manners meet their fight!

In a new world they wake, as from the dead ;   155

Yet doubt the trance diffolv'd, the vifion fled!

* —fallentis femita vitæ.   Hor.

O come,

O come, and, rich in intellectual wealth,

Blend thought with exercife, with knowledge health ;

Long, in this fhelter'd fcene of letter'd talk,

With fober ftep repeat the penfive walk ;   160

Nor fcorn, when graver triflings fail to pleafe,

The cheap amufements of a mind at eafe ;

Here every care in fweet oblivion caft,

And many an idle hour—not idly pafs'd.

No tuneful echoes, ambufh'd at my gate,   165

Catch the bleft accents of the wife and great. ''

Vain of its various page, no Album breathes

The figh that Friendfhip, or the Mufe bequeathes.

Yet fome good Genii o'er my hearth prefide,

Oft the far friend, with fecret fpell, to guide ;   170

And

And there I trace, when the grey evening lours,

A filent chronicle of happier hours!

 When Chriftmas revels in a world of fnow,

And bids her berries blufh, her carols flow;

His fpangling fhow'r when Froft the wizard flings,   175

Or, borne in ether blue on viewlefs wings,

O'er the white pane his filvery foliage weaves,

And gems with icicles the fheltering eaves;

—Thy muffled friend his nectarine-wall purfues,

What time the fun the yellow crocus wooes,   180

Screen'd from the arrowy North; and duly hies *

To meet the morning-rumour as it flies;

  * Fallacem circum, vefpertinumque pererro
   Sæpe forum.   Hor.

              To

To range the murmuring market-place, and view

The motley groups that faithful TENIERS drew.

When Spring burfts forth in bloffoms thro' the vale,   185

And her wild mufic triumphs on the gale,

Oft with my book I mufe from ftile to ftile; *

Oft in my porch the liftlefs noon beguile,

Framing loofe numbers, till declining day

Thro' the green trellis fhoots a crimfon ray;   190

Till the Weft-wind leads on the twilight hours,

And fhakes the fragrant bells of clofing flowers.

Thus, in this calm recefs, fo richly fraught

With mental light, and luxury of thought;

* Tantôt, un livre en main, errant dans les préries—   BOILEAU.

Thus

Thus, while the world but claims its proper part,   195

Oft in the head, but never in the heart,

My life fteals on; (O could it blend with thine!)

Carelefs my courfe, yet not without defign.

So thro' the vales of Loire the bee-hives glide, ''

The light raft dropping with the filent tide;   200

So, till the laughing fcenes are loft in night,

The bufy people wing their various flight,

Culling unnumber'd fweets from namelefs flowers,

That fcent the vineyard in its purple hours.

Rife, ere the watch-relieving clarions play,   205

Caught thro' St. James's groves at blufh of day;

Ere its full voice the choral anthem flings

Thro' trophied tombs of heroes and of kings.

Hafte

Hafte to the tranquil fhade of learned eafe, *

Tho' fkill'd alike to dazzle and to pleafe ;   210

Tho' each gay fcene be fearch'd with anxious eye,

Nor thy fhut door be pafs'd without a figh.

If, when this roof fhall know thy friend no more,

Some, form'd like thee, fhould once, like thee, explore;

Invoke the lares of his lov'd retreat,   215

And his lone walks imprint with pilgrim-feet;

Then be it faid, (as, vain of better days,

Some grey domeftic prompts the partial praife;)

" Unknown he liv'd, unenvied, not unbleft;

Reafon his guide, and Happinefs his gueft.   220

* Innocuas amo delicias doctamque quietem.

In

In the clear mirror of his moral page,

We trace the manners of a purer age.

His foul, with thirſt of genuine glory fraught,

Scorn'd the falſe luſtre of licentious thought.

—One fair aſylum from the world he knew,   225

One choſen feat, that charms with various view!

Who boaſts of more (believe the ſerious ſtrain)

Sighs for a home, and ſighs, alas! in vain.

Thro' each he roves, the tenant of a day,

And, with the ſwallow, wings the year away!" [18]   230

THE END.

D 2

N O T E S

A N D

I L L U S T R A T I O N S.

Note I. Verse 25.

Oft o'er the mead, at pleasing distance, pass—

Cosmo of Medicis preferred his Apennine villa, because all that he commanded from its windows was exclusively his own.

How unworthy of his character; and how unlike the wise Athenian, who, when he had a farm to sell, directed the cryer to proclaim, as its best recommendation, that it had a good neighbourhood!

Plut. in Vit. Themist.

Note II. Verse 35.

And, thro' the various year, the various day—

Horace commends the house,

—— longos quæ prospicit agros.

And I think he is right. Distant views, if there is a good foreground, are generally the most pleasing; as they contain the greatest variety, both in themselves, and in their accidental variations.

Mr. Gilpin on the High-Lands of Scotland, i. 159.

Note

Note III. Verse 61.

Small change of scene, small space his home requires—

Many a great man, in paffing through the apartments of his palace, has made the melancholy reflection of the venerable Cofmo: Quefta è troppo gran cafa à fi poca famiglia.   Mach. Ift. Fior. lib. vii.

I confefs, fays Cowley, I love littlenefs almoft in all things. A little convenient eftate, a little chearful houfe, a little company, and a very little feaft.   Effay vi.

So alfo fays the Conqueror of Silefia !

> Petit bien, qui ne doit rien,
>
> Petite maifon, petite table, &c.

When Socrates was afked why he had built for himfelf fo fmall a houfe, " Small as it is," he replied, " I wifh I could fill it with " friends."   Phædrus, l. iii. 9.

Thefe indeed are all that a wife man would defire to affemble ; " for a " croud is not company, and faces are but a gallery of pictures, and talk " but a tinkling cymbal, where there is no love."

              Bacon's Effays, xxvii.

Note IV. Verse 64.

From every point a ray of genius flows !

By this means, when the heavens are filled with clouds, when the earth fwims in rain, and all nature wears a lowering countenance, I withdraw

withdraw myfelf from thefe uncomfortable fcenes into the vifionary worlds of art; where I meet with fhining landfkips, gilded triumphs, beautiful faces, and all thofe other objeſts that fill the mind with gay ideas, &c. ADDISON.

It is remarkable that Antony, in his adverfity, paffed fome time in a fmall but fplendid retreat, which he called his Timonium, and from which probably originated the idea of the Parifian Boudoir, that favorite apartment, *ou l'on fe retire pour être feul, mais ou l'on ne boude point.*

STRABO, l. vii. PLUT. in Vit. Anton.

NOTE V. Verfe 79.
O mark! again the courfers of the Sun,
At GUIDO's call, &c.

Alluding to his celebrated frefco in the Rofpigliofi Palace at Rome. It has been engraved by Morghen.

NOTE VI. Verfe 87.
And ſtill the Few beſt lov'd and moſt rever'd—

The dining-room is dedicated to Conviviality; or, as Cicero fomewhere expreffes it, Communitati vitæ atque viſtûs. There we wifh moſt for the fociety of our friends; and, perhaps, in their abfence, moſt require their portraits.

The moral advantages of this furniture may be illuſtrated by the pretty ſtory of an Athenian courtezan, "who, in the midſt of a riotous banquet

with

with her lovers, accidentally caſt her eye on the portrait of a philoſopher, that hung oppoſite to her ſeat : the happy character of temperance and virtue ſtruck her with ſo lively an image of her own unworthineſs, that ſhe inſtantly quitted the room ; and, retiring home, became ever after an example of temperance, as ſhe had been before of debauchery."

WEBB's Inquiry into the Beauties of Painting, p. 33.'

NOTE VII.   Verſe 88.
Riſe round the board, &c.—

A long table, and a ſquare table, ſays Bacon, ſeem things of form, but are things of ſubſtance; for at a long table a few at the upper end, in effect, ſway all the buſineſs.   Eſſay xx.

Perhaps Arthur was right, when he inſtituted the order of the round table.   In the town-houſe of Aix-la-Chapelle is ſtill to be ſeen the round table, which may almoſt literally be ſaid to have given peace to Europe in 1748.   Nor is it only at a congreſs of plenipotentiaries that place gives precedence.

NOTE VIII.   Verſe 89.
Nor boaſt, O Choiſy, ſeat of ſoft delight—

At the petits ſoupés of Choiſy were firſt introduced thoſe admirable pieces of mechaniſm, afterwards carried to perfection by Loriot, the Confidente and the Servante ; a table and a ſide-board, which deſcended, and roſe again covered with viands and wines.   And thus the moſt luxurious

Court

Court in Europe, after all its boafted refinements, was glad to return at laft, by this fingular contrivance, to the quiet and privacy of humble life. Vie privée de Louis XV. tom. ii. p. 43.

NOTE IX. Verfe 94:

Sheds, like an evening-ftar, its ray ferene.

At a Roman fupper ftatues were fometimes employed to hold the lamps.

— Aurea funt juvenum fimulacra per ædcis,

Lampadas igniferas manibus retinentia dextris. LUCR. ii. 24.

A fafhion as old as Homer ! Odyff. vii. 100.

On the proper degree and diftribution of light we may confult a great mafter of effeft. Il lume grande, ed alto, e non troppo potente, farà quello, che renderà le particole de' corpi molto grate. Tratt. della Pittura di Lionardo da Vinci. c. xli.

Hence every artift requires a broad and high light. Michael Angelo ufed to work with a candle fixed in his hat. Condivi, Vita di Michelagn. Hence alfo, in a banquet-fcene, the moft picturefque of all poets has thrown his light from the cieling. Æneid. i. 730.

And hence the " ftarry lamps" of Milton, that

from the arched roof

Pendent by fubtle magic, ————

———————— yielded light

As from a fky. Paradife Loft. i. 726.

E NOTE

NOTE X. Verſe 108.

Read ancient books, or woo inſpiring dreams.

The reader will here remember that paſſage of Horace,

Nunc veterum libris, nunc ſomno, &c.

which was inſcribed by Lord Cheſterfield on the frieze of his library.

NOTE XI. Verſe 109.

And, when a ſage's buſt arreſts thee there—

Siquidem non ſolum ex auro argentove, aut certe ex ære in biblio-
thecis dicantur illi, quorum immortales animæ in iiſdem locis ibi loquun-
tur : quinimo etiam quæ non ſunt, finguntur, pariuntque deſideria non
traditi vultus, ſicut in Homero evenit. Quo majus (ut equidem arbi-
tror) nullum eſt felicitatis ſpecimen, quam ſemper omnes ſcire cupere,
qualis fuerit aliquis.   PLIN. Nat. Hiſt. xxxv. 2.

Cicero ſpeaks with great affection of a little ſeat under Ariſtotle in the
library of Atticus. Literis ſuſtentor & recreor ; maloque in illa tua
ſedecula, quam habes ſub imagine Ariſtotelis, ſedere, quàm in iſtorum
ſella curuli !   Ep. ad Att. iv. 10.

Nor ſhould we forget that Dryden uſed to draw inſpiration from the
" majeſtic face" of Shakſpeare ; and that a print of Newton was the only
ornament of the cloſet of Buffon. Ep. to Kneller. Voyage à Mont-
bart par Hérault de Séchelles.

In

In the chamber of a man of genius we
                                        write all down :
            Such and fuch pictures ;—there the window ;
            —————————————— the arrras, figures,
            Why, fuch, and fuch.   Cymbeline.

NOTE XII.   Verfe 113.

Which gathers round the Wife of every Tongue.

Quis tantis non gaudeat & glorietur hofpitibus, exclaims Petrarch.—
Spectare, etfi nihil aliud, certè juvat.—Homerus apud me mutus, immò
verò ego apud illum furdus fum. Gaudeo tamen vel afpectû folo, et
fæpé illum amplexus ac fufpirans dico: O magne vir, &c.

                                        Epift. Var. Lib.

NOTE XIII.   Verfe 128.

A fullen captive broods in filence there.

This thought is moft beautifully dilated in an Infcription for an Ice-
houfe, by a Lady of great celebrity in the Literary World. Nor has it
efcaped Waller in his verfes on St. James's Park. v. 53.

Note XIV. Verfe 137.

Thefe eyelids open to the rifing ray.

Your bed-chamber, and alfo your library, fays Vitruvius, fhould have an eaftern afpeft; ufus enim matutinum poftulat lumen.

Not fo the pifture-gallery; which requires a north-light, uti colores in ope, propter conftantiam luminis, immutata permaneant qualitate. L. vi. c. 6.

This difpofition accords with his plan of a Grecian houfe. L. vi. c. 9.

Note XV. Verfe 149.

Like thofe blefl Youths (forgive the fabling page)

See the Legend of the Seven Sleepers, as tranflated from the Syriac by the care of Gregory of Tours.   GIBBON's Hift. c. 33.

Note XVI. Verfe 166.

Catch the blefl accents of the wife and great.

Mr. Pope delights in enumerating his illuftrious guefts. Nor is this an exclufive privilege of the Poet. The Medici Palace at Florence exhibits a long and impofing catalogue. ' Semper hi parietes columnæque eruditis vocibus refonuerunt.'

Another is alfo preferved at Chanteloup, the feat of the Duke of Choifeul.

NOTE

NOTE XVII. Verſe 199.

So thro' the vales of Loire the bee-hives glide.

An alluſion to the floating bee-houſe, or barge laden with bee-hives, which Goldſmith ſays he ſaw in ſome parts of France and Piedmont.

Hiſt. of the Earth. viii. 87.

NOTE XVIII. Verſe 230.

And, with the ſwallow, wings the year away!

It was the boaſt of Lucullus that he changed his climate with the birds of paſſage.   Plut. in Vit. Lucull.

How often muſt he have felt the truth here inculcated, that the maſter of many houſes has no home!

TO A

FRIEND

ON HIS

MARRIAGE.

ON thee, bleſt youth, a father's hand confers

The maid thy earlieſt, fondeſt wiſhes knew.

Each ſoft enchantment of the ſoul is hers;

Thine be the joys to firm attachment due.

As on ſhe moves with heſitating grace,

She wins aſſurance from his ſoothing voice;

And, with a look the pencil could not trace,

Smiles thro' her bluſhes, and confirms the choice.

Spare

Spare the fine tremors of her feeling frame !

To thee fhe turns—forgive a virgin's fears !

To thee fhe turns with fureft, tendereft claim;

Weaknefs that charms, reluctance that endears!

At each refponfe the facred rite requires,

From her full bofom burfts the unbidden figh.

A ftrange myfterious awe the fcene infpires;

And on her lips the trembling accents die.

O'er her fair face what wild emotions play !

What lights and fhades in fweet confufion blend!

Soon fhall they fly, glad harbingers of day,

And fettled funfhine on her foul defcend !

Ah foon, thine own confeft, ecftatic thought!

That hand fhall ftrew each flinty path with flowers;

And thofe blue eyes, with mildeft luftre fraught,

Gild the calm current of domeftic hours!

F

A FAREWELL.

A

F A R E W E L L.

ONCE more, enchanting girl, adieu!

I muſt be gone, while yet I may.

Oft ſhall I weep to think of you ;

But here I will not, cannot ſtay.

The ſweet expreſſion of that face,

For ever ſhifting, yet the ſame,

Ah no, I dare not turn to trace.

It melts my ſoul, it fires my frame !

Yet

Yet give me, give me, ere I go,

One little lock of thofe fo bleft,

That lend your cheek a warmer glow,

And on your white neck love to reft.

—Say, when to kindle foft delight,

That hand has chanc'd with mine to meet,

How could its thrilling touch excite

A figh fo fhort, and yet fo fweet ?

O fay—but no, it muft not be.

Adieu, enchanting girl, adieu !

—Yet ftill, methinks, you frown on me ;

Or never could I fly from you.

TO THE

GNAT.

WHEN by the greenwood fide, at fummer eve,

Poetic vifions charm my clofing eye ;

And fairy-fcenes, that Fancy loves to weave,

Shift to wild notes of fweeteft Minftrelfy ;

'Tis thine to range in bufy queft of prey,

Thy feathery antlers quivering with delight,

Brufh from my lids the hues of heav'n away,

And all is Solitude, and all is Night !

—Ah now thy barbed fhaft, relentlefs fly,

Unfheaths it's terrors in the fultry air !

No

No guardian fylph, in golden panoply,

Lifts the broad fhield, and points the fparkling fpear.

Now near and nearer rufh thy whirring wings,

Thy dragon-fcales ftill wet with human gore :

Hark, thy fhrill horn its fearful larum flings !

—I wake in horror, and ' dare fleep no more!'

F I N I S.

www.ingramcontent.com/pod-product-compliance
Lightning Source LLC
Chambersburg PA
CBHW032136080426
42733CB00008B/1103